HAVING FUN WITH FEELINGS
ON THE AUTISM SPECTRUM

by the same authors

Exploring Depression, and Beating the Blues
A CBT Self-Help Guide to Understanding and Coping
with Depression in Asperger's Syndrome [ASD-Level I]
Tony Attwood and Michelle Garnett
ISBN 978 I 84905 502 4
eISBN 978 0 85700 907 4

CBT to Help Young People with Asperger's
Syndrome (Autism Spectrum Disorder) to
Understand and Express Affection
A Manual for Professionals
Tony Attwood and Michelle Garnett
ISBN 978 I 84905 412 6
eISBN 978 0 85700 801 5

From Like to Love for Young People with Asperger's
Syndrome (Autism Spectrum Disorder)
Learning How to Express and Enjoy
Affection with Family and Friends
Tony Attwood and Michelle Garnett
ISBN 978 I 84905 436 2
eISBN 978 0 85700 777 3

Having Fun with Feelings on the Autism Spectrum

A CBT Activity Book for Kids Age 4–8

Michelle Garnett, Tony Attwood, Louise Ford,
Stefanie Runham and Julia Cook

Jessica Kingsley Publishers
London and Philadelphia

First published in 2020
by Jessica Kingsley Publishers
73 Collier Street
London N1 9BE, UK
and
400 Market Street, Suite 400
Philadelphia, PA 19106, USA

www.jkp.com

Library of Congress Cataloging in Publication Data
A CIP catalog record for this book is available from the Library of Congress

British Library Cataloguing in Publication Data
A CIP catalogue record for this book is available from the British Library

ISBN 978 1 78775 327 3
eISBN 978 1 78775 328 0

Printed and bound in China

Happiness
Activity
Booklet

HAPPY HENRY THE HONEYDEW

Hi, I'm Happy Henry the Honeydew and I feel happy! When I'm happy, my eyes light up and my mouth has a great big smile, and sometimes I laugh. Being happy makes me feel so good inside. My body feels bouncy and full of energy! I feel happy playing with my friend or my favourite toy. I feel happy when I eat my favourite food, yoghurt. I feel happy when I go for a walk by the beach because it is fun! I like feeling happy. Seeing me happy makes other people feel happy too!

Just as people need tools to fix things like broken toys and dripping taps, we all need tools for dealing with some feelings, such as too much anger, sadness or worry. Today I have told you some of my Happy Tools, like being on the beach and playing with my favourite toys. Happy Tools are the things that make you feel happy. I would love to know your Happy Tools!

There are lots of types
of tools in a normal toolbox.
There are also lots of types of tools
in your Emotional Toolbox. One of the most
important tools in there is called an Awareness
Tool. Awareness means knowing. Your Awareness
Tools include knowing that you have feelings, knowing
what they look like and feel like, and even knowing that
you have tools that can help! Awareness Tools are some
of our most powerful ones — they are the power tools
in our Toolbox, like the electrical drill. To deal with a
feeling, you have to know it is there! And you cannot
use a tool that you didn't know you had! Knowledge
is very powerful. Together we are going to
become very smart about you, your
feelings and your tools.

HAPPY

We all feel different
levels of happy. Sometimes we are
a little happy. Sometimes we are happy.
Sometimes we are really happy. We can
rate how happy we are feeling on the
Happy Thermometer.

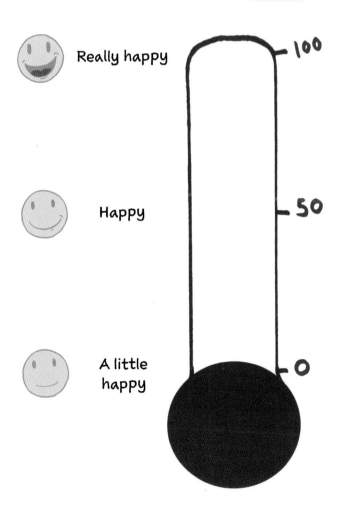

Really happy

Happy

A little
happy

100

50

0

On this page, look at the pictures of things that can make people 'a little happy', 'happy' and 'really happy'. Cut out the pictures of the things that make you happy and stick them on the 'a little happy', 'happy' and 'really happy' pages. Next, think of other things that make you happy and draw these on the 'a little happy', 'happy' and 'really happy' pages. You can look on the internet for more pictures of things that make you feel happy to add to the page.

Birthdays

Christmas

Going to the park

Watching TV

Playing on the iPad

Playing a game with my mum or dad

Seeing my grandparents

Playing with my pet

Playing with trains

Playing with dinosaurs

Playing with dolls

Swimming

WHAT MAKES ME FEEL REALLY HAPPY?

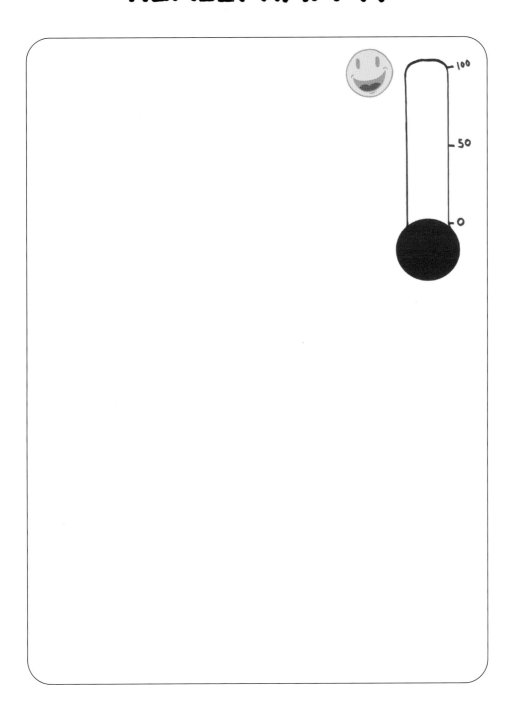

WHAT MAKES ME FEEL HAPPY?

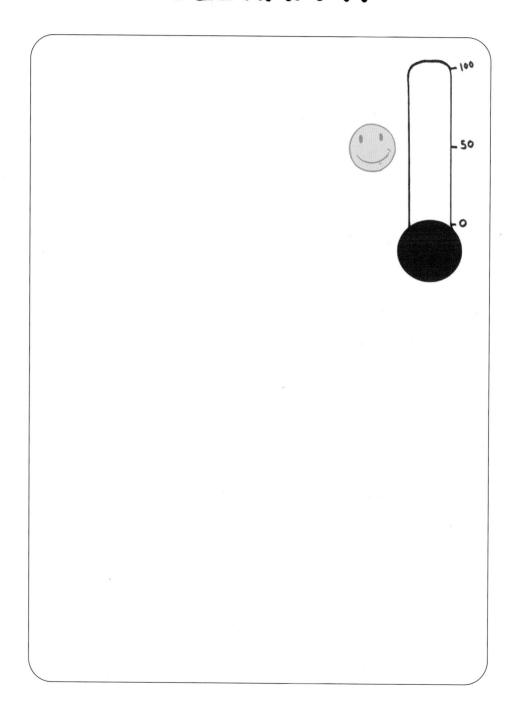

WHAT MAKES ME FEEL A LITTLE HAPPY?

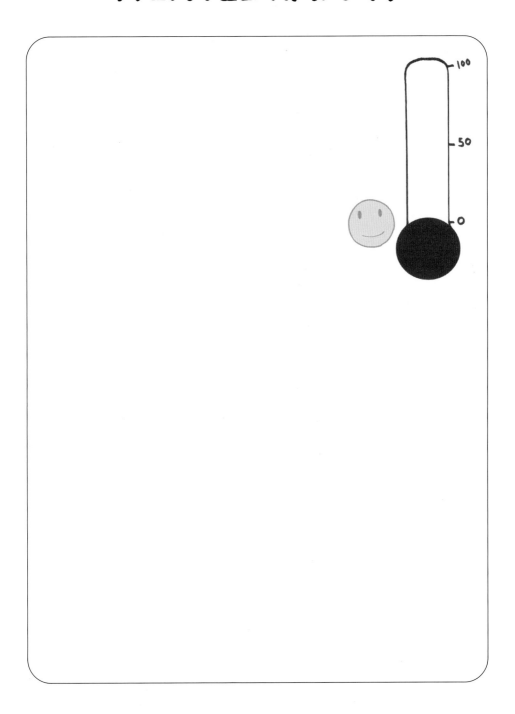

WE ARE ALL DIFFERENT

What makes you happy is different to what makes me happy. I feel happy when I roll in the mud. Does rolling in the mud make you happy too?

What is one thing that makes you happy and makes Mum or Dad happy too?

What is one thing that makes you happy but doesn't make Mum or Dad happy?

What is one thing that makes Mum and Dad happy but doesn't make you happy?

MR FACE

Mr Face doesn't know how to make a happy face on his own.
Can you help him to make a happy face? Draw a picture of his
happy face.

HAPPY BODY, HAPPY MIND

When did you feel really happy? What happened? Who was there? What did you hear? What did you see?

What did your body feel like when you were happy?

☐ Tingling and alive

☐ Light and buzzing

☐ Energizing, feel like jumping up and down, flapping my arms or hands

☐ Soft feelings in my arms, legs, tummy

☐ Good; my body feels good

☐ My tummy feels warm

It is time for a Happy Story.

Lie in a comfortable position. Now that you are comfortable, try to stay in that position and listen to my voice. Take in a breath [pause] and then breathe out. Aaaaaah. Now imagine you are getting into a spaceship to time-travel back to the time you felt really happy. The spaceship has landed and the door opens. You get in and press a red button. You are now back in time to when you felt really happy. You climb out of your spaceship and you feel so happy.

You can see _____ [the people or animals who were there].

You can hear _____.

You can see _____, smell _____, feel _____ [insert the details you collected earlier].

It is as if it is all happening again right now. You notice how your body is feeling.

Your body feels _____ [insert the information you collected earlier].

This is happiness. Happiness lives in your body. Whenever you wish to, you can bring back this memory of being happy and feel the feelings of being happy in your body. Now you climb back into the spaceship, bringing the feelings of happiness in your body with you. You press a green button. You are now back in the room, with your happy body feelings with you.

It was so great to meet you! Playing with you made me feel REALLY HAPPY. See you next time!

Sadness
Activity
Booklet

SAD SALLY THE STRAWBERRY

Hi, I'm Sad Sally the Strawberry and I feel sad. When I'm sad, my eyes look down, my face has a frown and sometimes I cry. Being sad makes my body feel heavy and droopy. I feel sad when my toy breaks or someone is mean to me or won't let me play. I feel sad when someone I care about goes away. I feel sad when my mum and dad won't let me do something I want to do. Feeling sad isn't a very nice feeling.

SAD

Everyone feels sad sometimes. Sometimes we are a little sad. Sometimes we are sad. Sometimes we are really sad. We can rate how sad we feel on the Sad Thermometer.

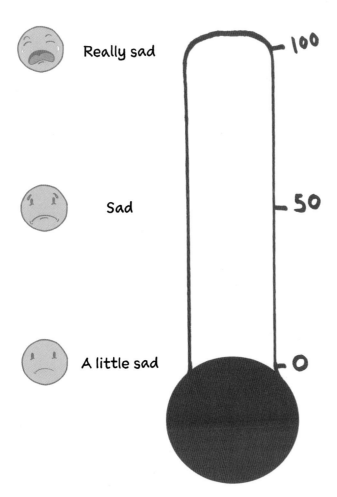

Really sad — 100

Sad — 50

A little sad — 0

Look at the pictures of things that can make people 'a little sad', 'sad', and 'really sad'. Cut out the pictures and choose the photographs of the things that make you sad. Stick them on the 'a little sad', 'sad', and 'really sad' pages. Next, think of other things that make you sad and draw these on the ' a little sad', 'sad', and 'really sad' pages. Here are some pictures of things that make some people sad.

Losing a toy

Being sick

Getting hurt

Saying goodbye to someone I love

Having no one to play with

Mum or Dad saying no

Someone being mean to me

My toy is broken

Having no one to talk to

Seeing someone else feeling sad

A pet dies

Watching a sad movie

WHAT MAKES ME FEEL REALLY SAD?

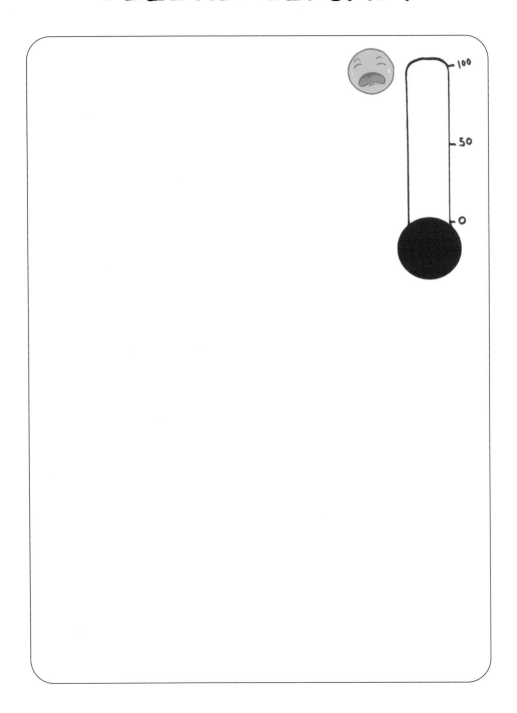

WHAT MAKES ME FEEL SAD?

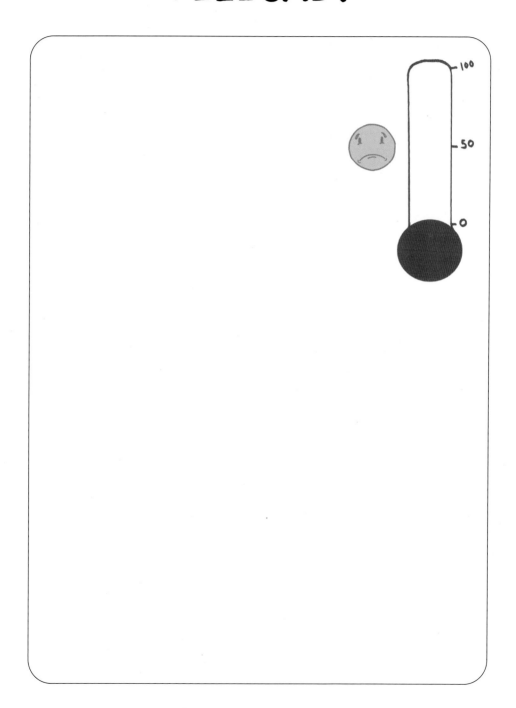

WHAT MAKES ME FEEL A LITTLE SAD?

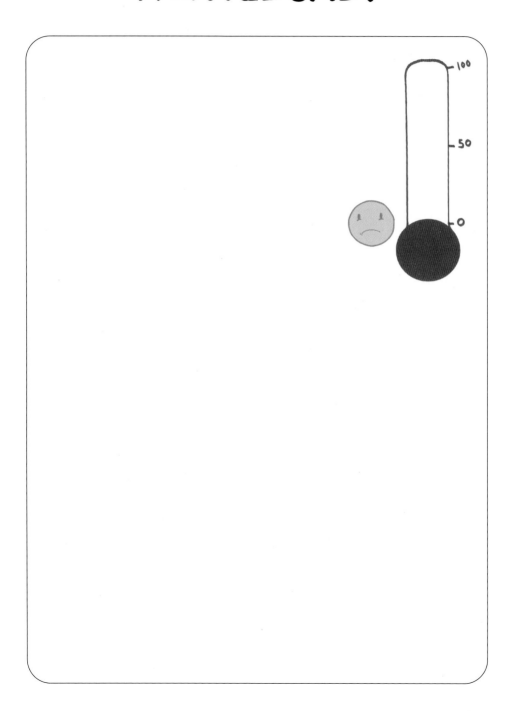

WE ARE ALL DIFFERENT

What makes you sad is different to what makes me sad. I feel sad when I have no one to talk to. Does having no one to talk to make you sad too?

What is one thing that makes you sad and makes Mum or Dad sad too?

What is one thing that makes you sad but doesn't make Mum or Dad sad?

What is one thing that makes Mum and Dad sad but doesn't make you sad?

MR FACE

Mr Face doesn't know how to make a sad face on his own. Can you help him to make a sad face? Draw a picture of his sad face.

SAD BODY, SAD MIND

Lie down or sit down and listen to this story. Imagine a time when you felt a little bit sad. Maybe it was because you were tired, or maybe it was just a bad day. Bring that time back into your mind now. While imagining this time, remember that it is just a memory, just a thought. It is not happening right now. As you think about this time, notice how your body feels. How does your face feel? Your tummy? Your arms? Your legs? Your throat? Your eyes? Now bring your thoughts back to here and now. Wriggle your toes and think of a happy or funny memory. Open your eyes and let's talk about what your body felt like when it was feeling a little bit sad.

Well done trying to imagine a time when you felt sad! That was hard! My body started to feel heavy and my eyes felt like crying. How did your body feel? Did you feel...

☐ Shaky

☐ Dark

☐ No energy, like you want to lie down and sleep

☐ Heavy feelings in your arms, legs, tummy

☐ Cold

☐ Like your heart was empty

Hi there, everyone! It's me again! When we were together last time, we explored Happy Tools. Today we are going to find out even more about Happy Tools. You can use these tools whenever you feel sad. You can even use them when you feel angry or worried.

HAPPY TOOLS

Let's find out more about Happy Tools! You will remember that Happy Tools are fun activities that I can do to help me feel happy and relaxed. Some of my Happy Tools are playing Lego, playing in the backyard and drawing pictures.

Look at the pictures of Happy Tools below. Circle the pictures of Happy Tools that you would like to use to help you feel happy and relaxed. Draw or write your own ideas for Happy Tools in the empty boxes.

Playing with trains	Playing in the backyard	Playing with dinosaurs
Reading	Drawing	Playing with dolls
Playing on the iPad	Looking at my collection	Watching TV
Building	Playing with my pet	Playing with my sensory toys

HAPPINESS TOOL CHART

This week we are going to practise using our Happy Tools. Use the Happiness Tool Chart to rate how happy you felt before and after using your Happy Tools. It is OK if you feel Sad after using a Happy Tool, this happens sometimes. If this happens, circle a sad face.

	Tool	Before	After
Monday			
Tuesday			
Wednesday			
Thursday			
Friday			
Saturday			
Sunday			

Have fun using your Happy Tools this week.
See you next time!

Worry
Activity
Booklet

WORRIED WANDA THE WATERMELON

Hi, I'm Worried Wanda the Watermelon and I feel worried.
When I feel worried, my eyes go wide, my eyebrows go up, my
lips start to shake and I put my hands on my face. When I feel
worried, my stomach has butterflies, my hands get all sweaty
and my legs become wobbly. I feel worried when someone I care
about is sick and when I think I might get into trouble. I feel
worried before I go on scary rides and if someone is mad at me.
I do not like feeling worried.

WORRIED

We all feel different
levels of worry. Sometimes we
are a little worried. Sometimes we are
worried. Sometimes we are really worried.
We can rate how worried we are feeling
on the Worry Thermometer.

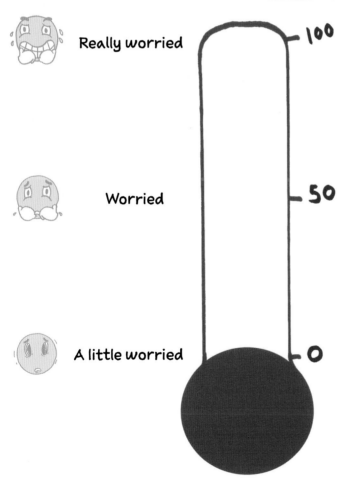

Really worried — 100

Worried — 50

A little worried — 0

WHAT MAKES ME FEEL REALLY WORRIED?

How can I tell when I am really worried? What do I do?

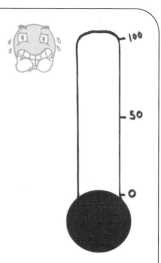

WHAT MAKES ME FEEL WORRIED?

How can I tell when I am worried?

What do I do?

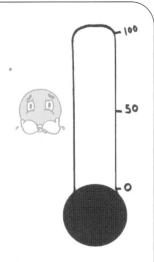

WHAT MAKES ME FEEL A LITTLE WORRIED?

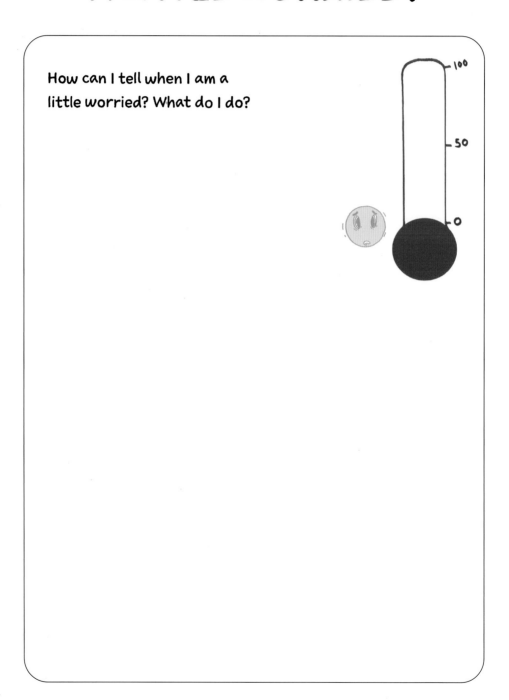

How can I tell when I am a little worried? What do I do?

WE ARE ALL DIFFERENT

What makes you worried is different to what makes me worried. I feel worried when people want to use me as a football. I am not a football! Does that make you worried too?

What is one thing that makes you worried and makes Mum or Dad worried too?

What is one thing that makes you worried but doesn't make Mum or Dad worried?

What is one thing that makes Mum or Dad worried but doesn't make you worried?

MR FACE

Mr Face doesn't know how to make a worried face. Can you show him how to make a worried face? Draw a picture of his worried face.

REALLY WORRIED BODY SIGNS

I know I am **really worried** when my
heart beats really fast, I feel shaky all over and
I start to cry. I feel sick in the tummy and I need to go to
the toilet. My muscles feel tense, especially my neck and
tummy. My hands get sweaty. My mouth feels dry.
I breathe more quickly. Sometimes I just freeze.
Sometimes I need to jiggle and fiddle.

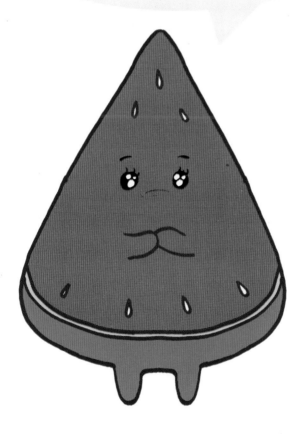

WORRIED BODY SIGNS ACTIVITY

I know I am **worried** when my muscles feel tense, especially in my tummy. My mouth feels dry. I feel like jiggling my legs. I fiddle with my toys.

WORRIED BODY SIGNS

Draw a line from each worried body sign to where it belongs in the body.

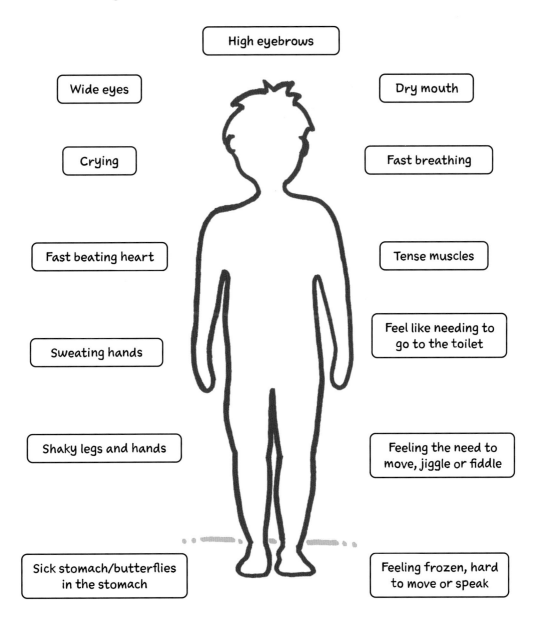

High eyebrows

Wide eyes

Dry mouth

Crying

Fast breathing

Fast beating heart

Tense muscles

Feel like needing to go to the toilet

Sweating hands

Shaky legs and hands

Feeling the need to move, jiggle or fiddle

Sick stomach/butterflies in the stomach

Feeling frozen, hard to move or speak

REAL ALARM

A real alarm is when there is real danger. Lots of changes happen in our bodies to prepare us to run away and fight. Worried Wanda the Watermelon had a real alarm when she accidentally rolled out on to the road and a car was coming and she was nearly squashed!

What are some real alarms for people?

FALSE ALARM

A false alarm is when there is no real danger but our bodies still want us to run away and fight. Worried Wanda the Watermelon had a false alarm when her teacher was away and she had to have a relief teacher.

What are some other false alarms people might have?

THOUGHT TOOLS

Thoughts are words
you say to yourself in your head.
When I am worried, I need to have Strong
Thoughts in my head to remind me that I can
be strong and I can be brave, even when
I don't feel those things.

I can be strong,
I can be brave and I can
cope. Sometimes when I am feeling
worried, I forget that I can do these things.
Remembering is helpful. I can write my Strong
Thoughts on cards to help me remember. My
Strong Thoughts are my Thought Tools.
Thought Tools work best when I am a
little worried or worried.

Let's make some Thought Tools for you. Write down your Strong Thoughts on cards and decorate the cards. Then you can read the cards whenever you start to feel a little worried.

I am smart

I am brave

I can try my best

Relaxation Activity Booklet

RELAXED RYAN THE RASPBERRY

Hi, I'm Relaxed Ryan the Raspberry and I feel relaxed. When I feel relaxed, my mouth smiles a small smile, my face is loose and sometimes I shut my eyes. When I feel relaxed, my body feels light and I feel as if I might float away. Sometimes I become so relaxed that I fall asleep! I feel relaxed after someone has read a nice story to me. I feel relaxed after I've had a bubble bath. I love feeling relaxed.

RELAXED

We all feel different
levels of relaxed. Sometimes we
are a little relaxed. Sometimes we are
relaxed. Sometimes we are really relaxed.
We can rate how relaxed we are on the
Relaxed Thermometer.

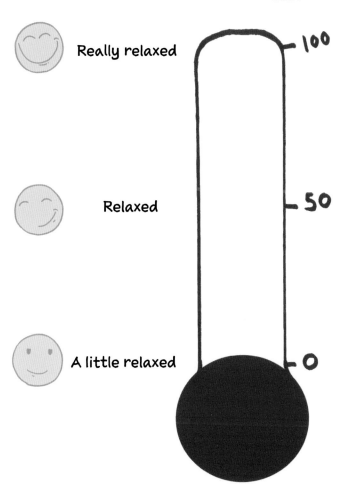

Really relaxed

Relaxed

A little relaxed

[AQ] Look at the pictures of things that can make people 'a little relaxed', 'relaxed' and 'really relaxed'. Cut out the pictures and choose the photographs of the things that make you happy. Stick them on the 'a little relaxed', 'relaxed' and 'really relaxed' pages. Next, think of other things that make you relaxed and draw these on the 'a little relaxed', 'relaxed' and 'really relaxed' pages. Here are some pictures of things that make some people relaxed.

Having a bath

Watching TV

Lying down at the beach

Hugging my teddy bear

Getting a massage

Sitting in a comfy chair

Hugging my pet

Playing a game with someone

Being alone

Listening to music

Sleeping

Lying down

WHAT MAKES ME FEEL REALLY RELAXED?

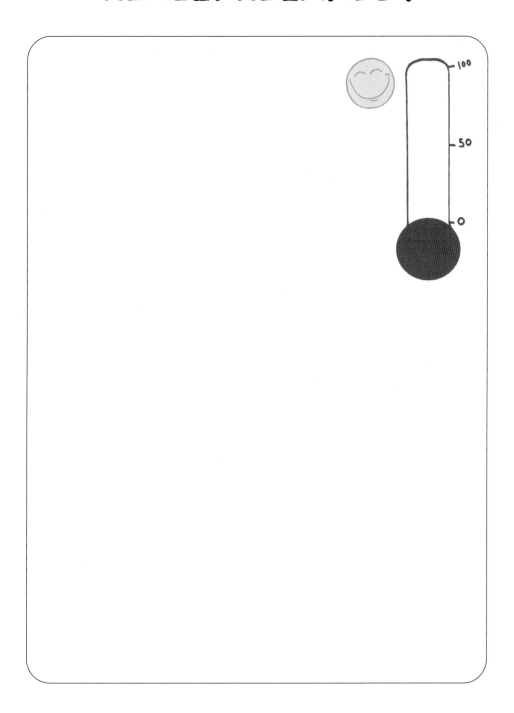

WHAT MAKES ME FEEL RELAXED?

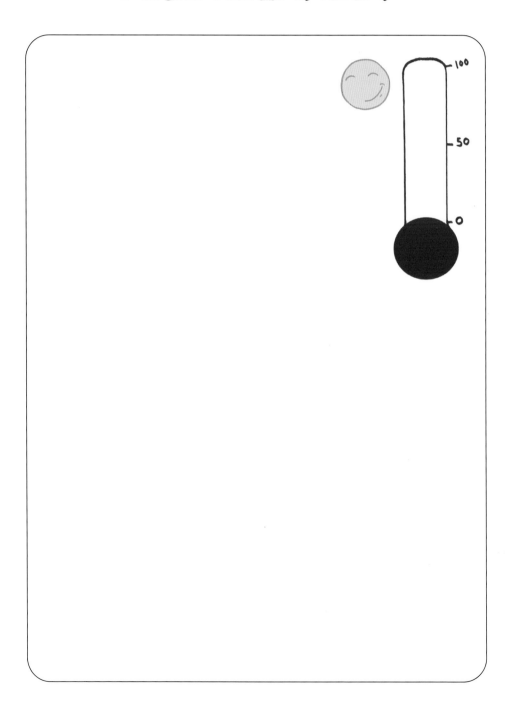

WHAT MAKES ME FEEL A LITTLE RELAXED?

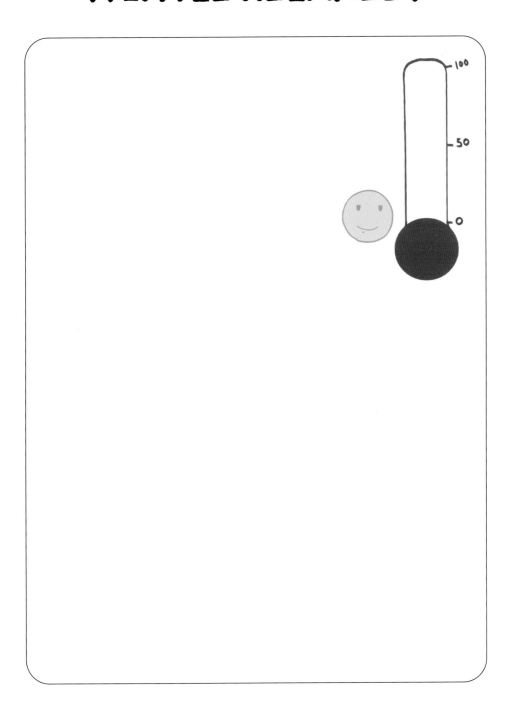

WE ARE ALL DIFFERENT

What makes me relaxed may be different to what makes you relaxed. I feel relaxed when I have a bath. Do you feel relaxed when you have a bath?

What is one thing that makes you relaxed and makes Mum or Dad relaxed too?

What is one thing that makes you relaxed but doesn't make Mum or Dad relaxed?

What is one thing that makes Mum and Dad relaxed but doesn't make you relaxed?

MR FACE

Mr Face doesn't know how to make a relaxed face on his own. Can you help him to make a relaxed face? Draw his relaxed face below.

RELAXED BODY SIGNS

Being relaxed makes my body feel slow and calm.

I know I am a little relaxed when I start to feel my muscles relax. My eyes and my jaw are soft. My breathing is slow too.

When I am relaxed, my tummy is calm and my heart is beating regularly. In fact, I can't even really feel my heart beating.

When I am really relaxed, my whole body feels flopping and heavy. I feel sleepy and like lying down.

RELAXED BODY SIGNS ACTIVITY

Draw a line from each relaxed body sign to where it belongs in the body.

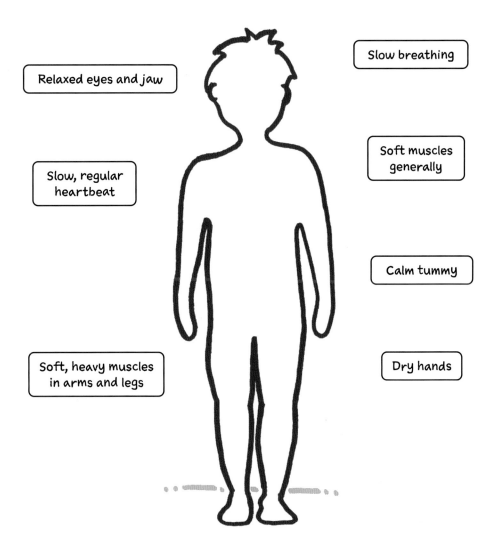

Relaxed eyes and jaw

Slow breathing

Slow, regular heartbeat

Soft muscles generally

Calm tummy

Soft, heavy muscles in arms and legs

Dry hands

RELAXATION TOOLS

Did you know that even I need some help to relax sometimes? Sometimes I get worried or too excited and I need to calm myself. Luckily, there are Relaxation Tools in my Toolkit! I do my special breathing, squeeze my muscles and use my imagination. These help my body and mind to feel relaxed. Do you want to learn how to use these Relaxation Tools?

SMELL THE FLOWER AND BLOW OUT THE CANDLE

1. Pretend you are holding a flower in your left hand.

2. Pretend you are holding a candle in your right hand.

3. Breathe in through your nose, pretending to smell the flower.

4. Breathe out through your mouth, pretending to blow out the candle.

DEFLATE THE BEACH BALL

1. Take a normal breath in through your nose.

2. Now imagine there is a giant inflatable beach ball in your tummy. Let all the air out of your ball slowly and steadily as you breathe out.

TAKE YOUR FAVOURITE TOY FOR A RIDE

1. Lie on your back on the floor.

2. Place your toy on top of your belly button.

3. Take a normal breath in while moving your tummy muscles out.

4. Let all the air out of your lungs slowly while moving your tummy muscles in.

5. Keep practising and watch to see whether your toy moves up and down.

TENSED AND RELAXED MUSCLES

When I want to relax,
I make juice to tense and
relax my muscles.

What juice should
we make today? Let's start by
making orange juice. Then you can
make any juice you want!

Recipe for Making Juice

* Let's make orange juice! Yum!
* Let's start with making juice with our feet!
* Take your two pretend oranges and place one underneath each foot.
* Breathe in.
* Curl your toes up and squeeze the orange for 1, 2, 3.
* Breathe out, relax, and let go of the oranges.
* Now take an orange and put it between your knees.
* Breathe in.
* Push your knees together and squeeze for 1, 2, 3.
* Breathe out, relax, and let go of the orange.
* Now put an orange on your tummy.
* Breathe in.
* Pull your tummy in and squeeze for 1, 2, 3.
* Breathe out, relax, and let go of the orange.
* Now hold an orange in each hand.
* Breathe in.
* Squeeze those oranges for 1, 2, 3.
* Breathe out, relax, and let go of the oranges.
* Hold both of your arms in front of you and put an orange between your elbows.
* Push your arms together and squeeze for 1, 2, 3.
* Breathe out, relax, and let go of the orange.
* Now put an orange on your back between your shoulder blades.
* Push your shoulder blades together and squeeze for 1, 2, 3.
* Breathe out, relax, and let go of the orange.
* Put an orange in your mouth.
* Squeeze down on the orange with your mouth for 1, 2, 3.
* Breathe out, relax, and let go of the orange.
* What juice will you make now? How many fruits can you squeeze?

IMAGINATION

Shut your eyes and imagine you are on a beach, or look at a picture of the beach. Imagine the sounds — seagulls calling, leaves blowing in the wind, waves crashing on the sand. Imagine the smells — the smell of the salty sea. Imagine the warm sun and breeze on your face, and the grainy sand as you lie on the beach. As you think of the beach, notice how calm and relaxed you are feeling. This is a special calming place you can imagine to relax.

RELAXATION TOOLS CHART

This week we are going
to practise using our Relaxation Tools.
Get Mum or Dad's help to rate how relaxed
and worried you feel before and after
using your Relaxation Tools.

	Tool	Before	After
Monday			
Tuesday			
Wednesday			
Thursday			
Friday			
Saturday			
Sunday			

Anger
Activity
Booklet

ANGRY ALAN THE APPLE

Hi, I'm Angry Alan the Apple and I feel angry. When I feel angry, my eyebrows go down, my forehead gets wrinkly and I grit my teeth. When I feel angry, my face goes red, my body feels tight, my hands want to punch, and my feet want to kick and stomp. I feel angry when someone takes my toy without asking. I feel angry when I want something and I'm not allowed to have it. I feel angry when someone tells me I'm wrong or I make a mistake. Feeling angry is not much fun. When I feel angry, I sometimes explode like a volcano and this can make other people feel scared and upset.

ANGRY

We all feel different
levels of being angry. Sometimes
we are a little angry. Sometimes we
are angry. Sometimes we are really angry.
We can rate how angry we are feeling
on the Angry Thermometer.

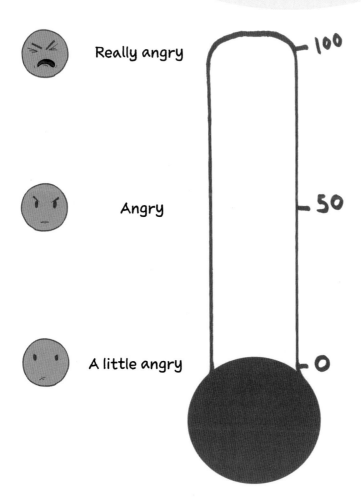

Really angry — 100

Angry — 50

A little angry — 0

WHAT MAKES ME FEEL REALLY ANGRY?

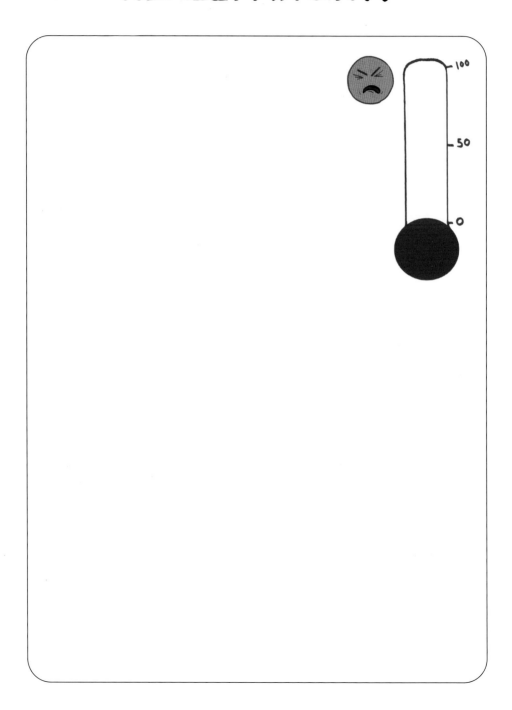

WHAT MAKES ME FEEL ANGRY?

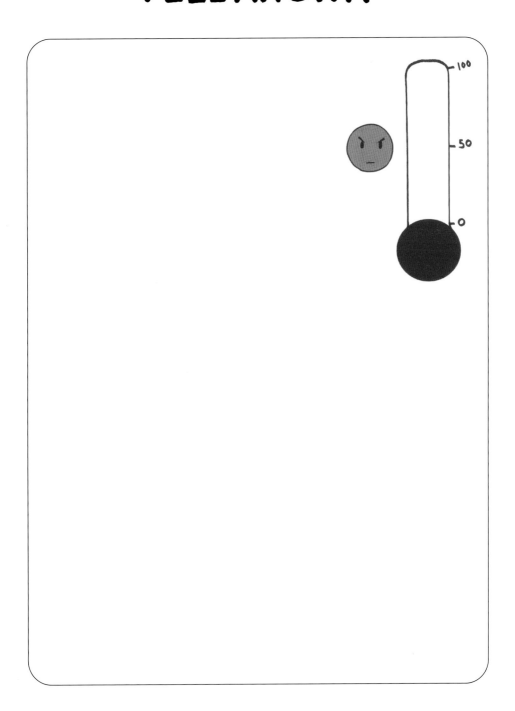

WHAT MAKES ME FEEL A LITTLE ANGRY?

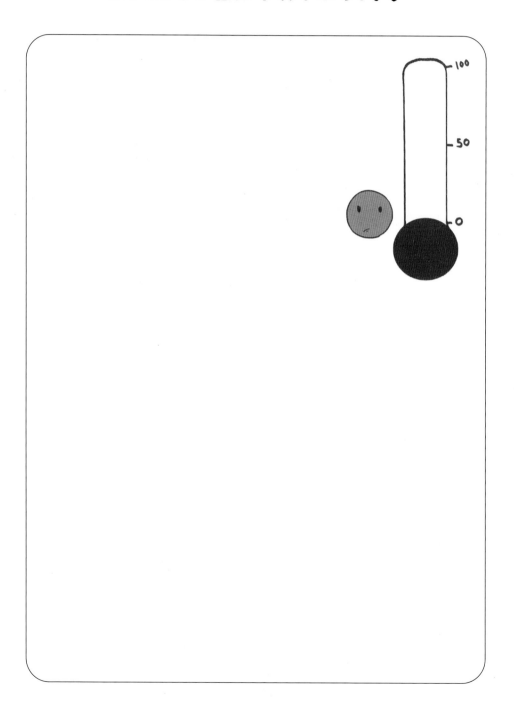

WE ARE ALL DIFFERENT

What makes you angry is different to what makes me angry. I feel angry when a worm tells me he prefers to eat bananas. How fussy! Does that make you angry too?

What is one thing that makes you angry and makes Mum or Dad angry too?

What is one thing that makes you angry but doesn't make Mum or Dad angry?

What is one thing that makes Mum or Dad angry but doesn't make you angry?

MR FACE

Mr Face doesn't know how to make an angry face. Can you show him how to make an angry face? Draw a picture of his angry face.

ANGRY BODY SIGNS

I know I am a little angry when I start to feel my muscles tense. My hands sometimes curl into fists. I grit my teeth.

When I am angry, my voice becomes loud, and my forehead gets wrinkly because I frown. Sometimes my eyebrows go down. I start to feel more energy in my body. I feel like moving.

When I am really angry, I feel hot and my face goes red. My fists want to punch, my legs want to kick, and my feet want to stomp. My heart beats faster.

ANGRY BODY SIGNS ACTIVITY

Draw a line from each angry body sign to where it belongs in the body.

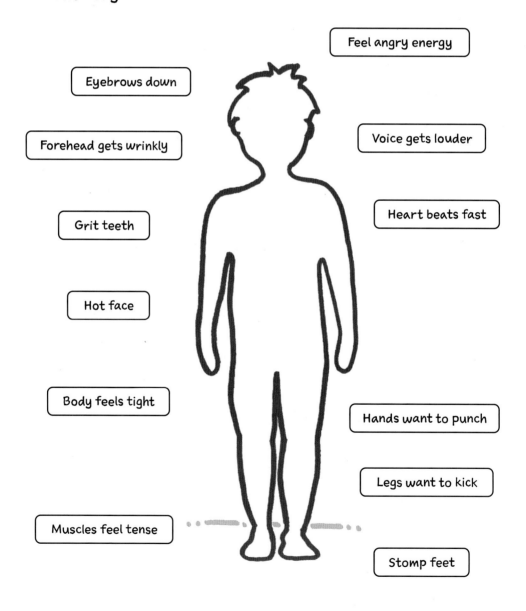

Feel angry energy

Eyebrows down

Forehead gets wrinkly

Voice gets louder

Grit teeth

Heart beats fast

Hot face

Body feels tight

Hands want to punch

Legs want to kick

Muscles feel tense

Stomp feet

EVERYDAY PHYSICAL TOOLS

I have a body that gets angry sometimes. Anger gives me a lot of energy. It helps me to burn off that energy every day. On days that I burn energy, I get less angry and I worry less. I feel happy, strong and confident. Every day I choose a different energy-burning tool – I call these my Everyday Physical Tools. My favourites are: bouncing on a trampoline, swinging on a swing and dancing with my favourite music on. What are your favourite Everyday Physical Tools?

USING EVERYDAY PHYSICAL TOOLS

Riding a bike

Riding a scooter

Swimming

Jumping on a trampoline

Dancing

Running around the backyard

Playing on playground equipment

Throwing a ball

Playing a team sport like soccer or baseball

Dance classes

Individual or group classes (e.g. tennis lesson, soccer skills lesson)

Draw your own:

ANGER BUSTING PHYSICAL TOOLS

When I am really angry, I need a Physical Tool to burn off the angry energy straight away. I like to swing on a swing or have a bounce in the garden. Afterwards I feel calmer and I am smarter. I call these my Anger-Busting Physical Tools. What activities help you to get the angry energy out? Circle the ways you can move to get the angry energy out straight away. Use the blank spaces to draw any other safe and quick ways you can get the anger out of your body.

Pillow punching

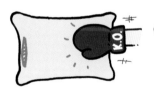

Throw a ball as far as you can

Crush empty cardboard boxes

Kick a ball

Run around the backyard

Swim

Jump up and down

Squeeze teddy
really tight

Jump on a trampoline

Squeeze a stress ball

EVERYDAY PHYSICAL TOOLS CHART

This week we are going
to practise using our Everyday Anger Tools
and our Anger-Busting Physical Tools. Get Mum
or Dad's help to rate how angry you felt before and
after using your Anger Tools. If you feel relaxed
afterwards, rate that too.

	Tool	Before	After
Monday			
Tuesday			
Wednesday			
Thursday			
Friday			
Saturday			
Sunday			

Like and
Love Activity
Booklet

LOVING LULU THE LEMON

Hi, I'm Loving Lulu the Lemon. There are many people and animals that I like and some that I love. I like my friends, and I really like my best friends, Banana and Gooseberry. I like all my Feeling Friends, Henry, Sally, Ryan, Wanda and Alan. I love my teddy bear, Boo. I also love my mum and dad. It feels great to like and love my friends and family. When I feel the emotion 'liking', I feel both relaxed and happy at the same time. My face is soft and open-looking. I look friendly. When I feel the emotion 'loving', I feel the same as liking, but more strongly. I also feel safe. My teddy and my mum and dad feel happy when I show them that I love them. When they are happy, I feel happy."

LIKE AND LOVE

We all feel like and love for people at different levels. Sometimes we like people only a little. Sometimes we like them, and sometimes we feel love for them. We can rate how much like or love we feel on the Like and Love Thermometer.

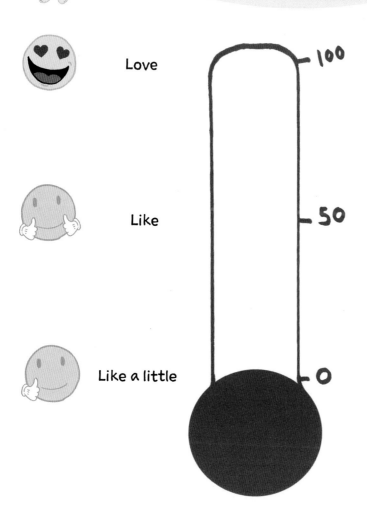

Love

Like

Like a little

100

50

0

WHAT MAKES ME FEEL LOVE?

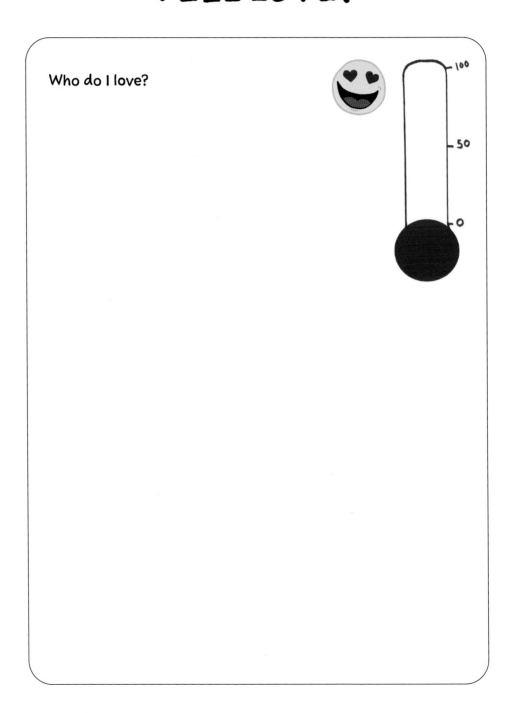

Who do I love?

WHAT MAKES ME FEEL LIKE?

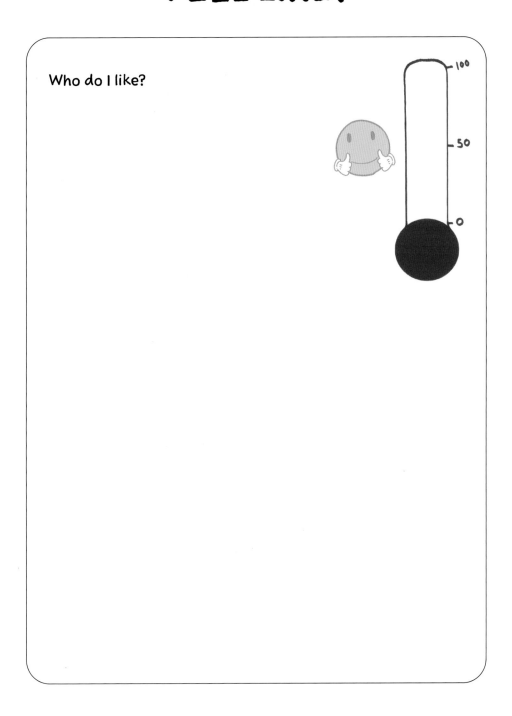

Who do I like?

WHAT MAKES ME FEEL A LITTLE LIKE?

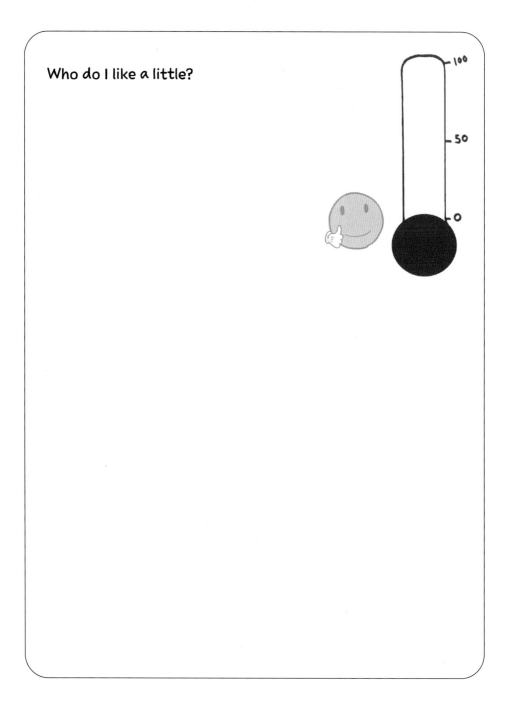

Who do I like a little?

WE ARE ALL DIFFERENT

What you like/love
is different to what I like/love.
I like when my pet sits on my lap.
Do you like that too?

What is one thing that you like/love and Mum or Dad
like/love too?

What is one thing that you like/love but Mum or Dad don't?

What is one thing that Mum or Dad like/love but you don't?

MR FACE

Mr Face doesn't know how to make a face to show that he likes someone. Can you help him to make a face that shows like? Draw a picture of this face.

BODY SIGNS OF LIKING SOMEONE

I really like my friend, Ryan the Raspberry. When I see Ryan, or even think about him, I can feel my face becoming soft and relaxed. My mouth feels relaxed. I feel relaxed, but I can feel my body has energy. It is a calm energy. I feel like playing and being creative. My hands are relaxed. My legs feel comfortable. I can sense that I am safe when I am with Ryan. This is the feeling of liking someone.

LIKE BODY SIGNS ACTIVITY

When we notice we like someone, our bodies tell us by relaxing around that person. Feeling liking for someone feels a bit like feeling relaxed. Draw lines between the body signs for liking someone, and the part of the body that feels that way.

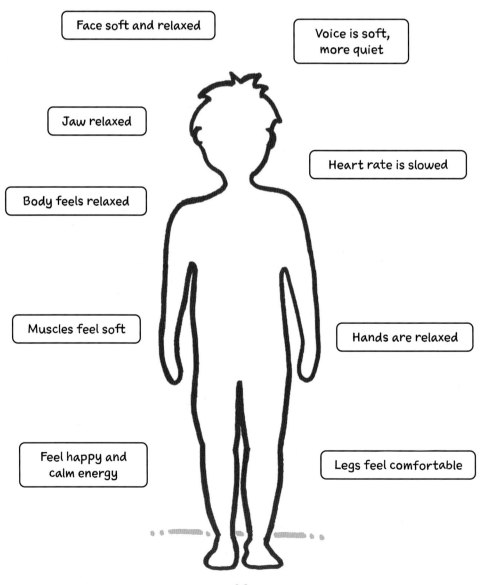

Face soft and relaxed

Voice is soft, more quiet

Jaw relaxed

Heart rate is slowed

Body feels relaxed

Muscles feel soft

Hands are relaxed

Feel happy and calm energy

Legs feel comfortable

SOCIAL TOOLS

When I feel worried or sad, I need to use my Social Tools to help me to feel better. Social Tools can be asking for help and spending time with people. I can also tell people who care about me how I am feeling.

There are people who love and like me. I can spend time with the people and animals in my life who help me to feel better. I like spending time with these people. It makes me feel liked and loved. When I am feeling liked or loved, I no longer feel worried or sad.

People who like and love me want me to feel happy. I can ask them for help when I need it. Asking for help is the smart thing to do. Then there are two brains working on the problem, not just one.

I can tell people who care about me how I am feeling. It is a strange thing, but when people agree that it is OK to feel angry, worried or sad, it helps. I feel better when people understand how I feel. They can then help me by reminding me that I can use the tools in my Emotional Toolbox.

WHO DO I LOVE AND LIKE?

On this page there are pictures of people you may like or love. Please circle the people you like or love. Use the blank spaces to draw other people of animals that you like or love.

My parents

My grandparents

My friend

My teacher

My pet

Other people

MY SOCIAL TOOLS

Tool 1: I can ask for help. Think of a time when you felt worried. Who could you ask for help? What would you say? Write the words in the speech bubble.

Tool 2: I can spend time playing with someone I like. Who would you choose? What would you say to that person?

Tool 3: I could tell someone who likes or loves me how I am feeling. Who would you choose? What would you say?

Thank you for having fun with us, your Feelings! We know we are not always fun. You have shown that you are strong and brave and smart by meeting and getting to know all of us. By getting to know us, your Feelings, and the tools in your Toolbox, you will be able to repair your feelings whenever you need to.

There is some secret knowledge that we have not yet told you. This secret will help you a lot.

When Angry Alan visits, Loving Lulu can be his best friend.

When Sad Sally comes, Happy Henry can really help.

Relaxed Ryan really knows how to help Worried Wanda.

Goodbye, Brave One, and always remember:
your Feelings are your Friends!